Samuel French Acting Edition

No. 6

by TJ Young

SAMUELFRENCH.COM   SAMUELFRENCH.CO.UK

Copyright © 2017 by TJ Young
All Rights Reserved

NO. 6 is fully protected under the copyright laws of the United States of America, the British Commonwealth, including Canada, and all other countries of the Copyright Union. All rights, including professional and amateur stage productions, recitation, lecturing, public reading, motion picture, radio broadcasting, television and the rights of translation into foreign languages are strictly reserved.

ISBN 978-0-573-70649-3

www.SamuelFrench.com
www.SamuelFrench.co.uk

FOR PRODUCTION ENQUIRIES

UNITED STATES AND CANADA
Info@SamuelFrench.com
1-866-598-8449

UNITED KINGDOM AND EUROPE
Plays@SamuelFrench.co.uk
020-7255-4302

Each title is subject to availability from Samuel French, depending upon country of performance. Please be aware that *NO. 6* may not be licensed by Samuel French in your territory. Professional and amateur producers should contact the nearest Samuel French office or licensing partner to verify availability.

CAUTION: Professional and amateur producers are hereby warned that *NO. 6* is subject to a licensing fee. Publication of this play(s) does not imply availability for performance. Both amateurs and professionals considering a production are strongly advised to apply to Samuel French before starting rehearsals, advertising, or booking a theatre. A licensing fee must be paid whether the title(s) is presented for charity or gain and whether or not admission is charged. Professional/Stock licensing fees are quoted upon application to Samuel French.

No one shall make any changes in this title(s) for the purpose of production. No part of this book may be reproduced, stored in a retrieval system, or transmitted in any form, by any means, now known or yet to be invented, including mechanical, electronic, photocopying, recording, videotaping, or otherwise, without the prior written permission of the publisher. No one shall upload this title(s), or part of this title(s), to any social media websites.

For all enquiries regarding motion picture, television, and other media rights, please contact Samuel French.

MUSIC USE NOTE

Licensees are solely responsible for obtaining formal written permission from copyright owners to use copyrighted music in the performance of this play and are strongly cautioned to do so. If no such permission is obtained by the licensee, then the licensee must use only original music that the licensee owns and controls. Licensees are solely responsible and liable for all music clearances and shall indemnify the copyright owners of the play(s) and their licensing agent, Samuel French, against any costs, expenses, losses and liabilities arising from the use of music by licensees. Please contact the appropriate music licensing authority in your territory for the rights to any incidental music.

IMPORTANT BILLING AND CREDIT REQUIREMENTS

If you have obtained performance rights to this title, please refer to your licensing agreement for important billing and credit requirements.

NO. 6 was first produced by the Texas State University Lab Theatre in San Marcos, Texas from April 14–17, 2016 under the direction of Carly Conklin. The cast was as follows:

ELLA	Jordan Ford
FELICIA	Emily Cross
FELIX	Anthony Hinderman
KELLY	Chris Clark

CHARACTERS

ELLA – Fifties. Female. African-American. Protective. Single mother.

FELICIA – Twenty-four. Female. African-American. Asperger's. High-functioning. Twin.

FELIX – Twenty-four. Male. African-American. Frustrated. Twin.

KELLY – Thirties. Male. White. Stubborn. Hiding a damning secret.

Scene One

(April 11, 2001. Cincinnati, Ohio.)

(Lights up on a small apartment. There is a worn-in sofa from the late eighties, along with a Lay-Z-Boy recliner in better condition than the couch. They form an eating area around a television, which, like most things in the space, is at least five to ten years old. It works, but there is a new digital antenna on top instead of bunny ears. Opposite of the seating area is a tiny kitchen table and a couple mismatched wooden chairs. The table has a stack of papers, a mix of junk mail and bills, and a few dinosaur books sit in front of one of the chairs. There is a small, battery-powered radio as well. A stack of R&B CDs sits beside the radio. On the back of the chairs, as well as hanging from random places throughout the apartment, are clothes that have been dry-cleaned and are in plastic bags. They have pink and yellow tags attached to them.)

(A single window is dressed modestly with discount store curtains and set in the wall next to the kitchen table. It is dark outside, but there is a faint yellow and sometimes orange glow through the window. A siren is heard passing by the window, and the space is filled with red and blue lights as a cop car passes up the street. Just past the window is an exit that leads to the kitchen and bedrooms.)

(There is a front door that leads into the apartment. Next to the front door is a small coat closet.)

*(In front of the television sits **FELICIA**, a black girl, twenty-four years old. She is wearing a kids' dinosaur watch. She stares at it, listening to the news report. She looks on with the intensity that a child has while watching Saturday morning cartoons.)*

REPORTER. *(Voice-over.)* – The crows are starting to assemble once again as police move into position. As the unrest stretches into its third night, it is still unclear as to when or if the city authorities can get the situation under control.

*(**ELLA**, a strong and soulful black woman in her early fifties, enters from the kitchen, rag in hand. She stands, watching the TV from across the room, shaking her head.)*

ELLA. Why you watchin' that stuff, girl? Ain't gonna do you no good.

FELICIA. But, it's just…thirteen blocks away, Mamma.

ELLA. It's been thirteen blocks away since yesterday. Turn it off.

FELICIA. Yesterday they started seventeen blocks away. The day before that was twenty-three. They movin' closer.

ELLA. They all the way on Spring. Long ways from us.

FELICIA. Not that long. Thirteen blocks.

ELLA. Turn it off.

FELICIA. From what I see, they are most likely going to cut across town. I wanna see how quickly they are moving. This is the only place I can get all the needed facts, Mamma. All the factors.

ELLA. I ain't sayin' it again. Turn it off and go wake up your brother.

*(**FELICA** turns the TV off. She stands.)*

FELICIA. Felix isn't here.

ELLA. Excuse me?

FELICIA. Felix isn't here. He left about...

>   *(She looks at her watch.)*

Forty-nine minutes ago.

ELLA. Don't that boy know curfew has been in place for over two hours?

FELICIA. I asked him the same thing. I told him the curfew was at six. He said that it didn't matter when curfew was if we didn't have food in the house. He went to go get us some.

ELLA. And he wasn't gonna say nothin' to me? You either?

FELICIA. Technically, he told me not to tell you. But you asked, so...

ELLA. That boy ain't thinkin' most of the time. The hell he doing out there... Like we ain't never gone without food for one night.

FELICIA. This will be our second day without food.

ELLA. A few days without eatin' ain't never hurt nobody. Look at it as an unplanned fast. Get you both right with the Lord. We use to have to fast with your grandma.

>   *(**ELLA** motions to some of the clothes draped around the apartment.)*

Move these out of the way, will ya? And hand me my smokes in the kitchen. They're next to the stove.

>   *(**FELICIA** grabs a few of the clothes and moves them over to the couch. **FELICIA** exits.)*

Yeah, that's fine. Just lay 'em right there.

>   *(**ELLA** reaches over, clicking on the radio. Soft jazz pours out of the speakers. She closes her eyes for a moment.)*

Your brother ain't thinkin' most of the time. Going out there with all them folks acting the way they are.

> (**FELICIA** *enters, cigarettes in hand. She takes one out of the box and hands it to her mother.*)

FELICIA. You said so yourself that they were a far ways off.

ELLA. From us. They a far ways off from us. Where is the nearest store, huh? Four blocks away? Four blocks closer than where we are. Besides, if he assumes some other folks haven't already cleaned out everything worth a damn, he's stupid.

FELICIA. He said he was gonna go down to the Jones' store, on Fillmore.

ELLA. He ain't goin' to the Jones' store. We both know they been closed for months now. He just lyin' to you so you won't worry.

FELICIA. I'm not worried. He said he would be safe. I trust him to be safe.

> (*The radio breaks away from the music, giving way to the* **DJ**'s *voice.*)

DJ. (*Voice-over.*) Breaking news from the riot building. Numbers much larger than the past two days have started to form in multiple parts of the city, stretching the local police department –

> (**ELLA** *reaches over and cuts the radio off.*)

ELLA. Jesus. Can't escape this crap. It's one thing to live it, but to hear it all the time… Give me some Coltrane and leave all the news crap for the TV.

> (**ELLA** *takes a long drag from her cigarette.* **FELICIA** *moves to the seat with the books in front of it. She cracks one open with the same intensity with which she watched the TV.*)

Any news from that one school? The one in Chicago?

FELICIA. Not yet. It's only been a month or so, Mamma. Plus, the mail hasn't been running like it normally does the past few days.

ELLA. Didn't you apply online?

FELICIA. They still send information by mail.

ELLA. Isn't that a bit prehistoric?

> (**ELLA** *laughs at her own joke.* **FELICIA** *looks at her. She doesn't find it funny.* **ELLA** *waves her off.*)

Come on. Don't you just love your mamma's jokes?

FELICIA. Love isn't the word I'd use. Sometimes, they're good. But most of the time, I'd say otherwise.

> (**ELLA** *ashes her cigarette. She reaches into her pocket, pulling out a flip cell phone.*)

ELLA. Call your brother, will ya?

FELICIA. Lines are most likely jammed.

ELLA. Why I gotta ask you twice to do somethin'? Call your brother, okay?

> (*She slides the phone over to* **FELICIA.** *Without looking up from her book,* **FELICIA** *grabs the phone from the table. She searches through the phone, finds Felix's number. Placing the phone up to her ear for a second, she listens, then flips it closed.*)

FELICIA. Lines are jammed.

> (**FELICIA** *slides the phone back to her mother.* **ELLA** *catches it, with a thin layer of patience, and slides it back to* **FELICIA.**)

ELLA. Try it again. Sometimes, you just gotta be persistent.

FELICIA. Can I wait for a few seconds?

ELLA. Jesus, girl. Your mamma tells you to try again, you just try again!

FELICIA. Yes, ma'am.

> (**FELICIA** *tries again. She flips the phone closed, sliding it back.*)

Still jammed.

ELLA. Why the hell do we even pay for these things, huh? They are supposed to be good for emergencies. We smack dab in the middle of one and we can't even reach no one. Heaven forbid we get broke into.

FELICIA. We won't. Store is boarded up.

ELLA. You think a few pieces of particle board really gonna stop someone from breakin' in downstairs if they really want to?

FELICIA. What could they want from a dry cleaners?

ELLA. Why they smash the windows at that pet store on Broadway? Them dogs and lizards and fish didn't do nothin' to those people. That place was black-owned, too.

FELICIA. Maybe they wanted a puppy.

ELLA. How they gonna feed a puppy right now?

FELICIA. IF they were smart, they would steal dog food, too.

>   (**FELICIA** *snaps her head up.*)

You heard anything about the Museum Center?

ELLA. What?

FELICIA. The museum! The Cincinnati Museum Center, specifically, the Museum of Natural History and Science.

ELLA. Girl, no one wants to break into the museum. They ain't tryin' to learn while they loot.

FELICIA. It's one of the few places in the country with an Allosaurus on display! It's beyond valuable!

ELLA. I'm sure they don't know that. No one else in this whole city knows them bones like you do, and if anyone does they most likely have enough common sense about them to stay inside. Unlike your knucklehead brother. I swear, I only gave birth to so much common sense at one time and you got most of it.

>   (**ELLA** *puts out her cigarette. She stares at her cell phone, tapping the outside of it with her finger.*)
>
>   (**FELICIA** *tries to go back to her book. The sound distracts her. She looks at her mom, seeing the worry on her face.* **FELICIA** *extends her hand.*)

FELICIA. I'll try again. Only if I can call Dr. Marshall if the lines are cleared.

> (**ELLA** *hands* **FELICIA** *the phone.*)

ELLA. Don't be wastin' all my minutes now, okay?

> (**FELICIA** *calls. She gets through this time.*)

FELICIA. Felix. Mamma said – Uh-huh. Okay.

ELLA. Where the hell is that boy?

FELICIA. Mamma wants to know where the hell you are.

> (*To* **ELLA**.)

He said he is a few blocks away. Moving a bit slow. Avoidin' the major roads.

ELLA. Did he get what he wanted?

FELICIA. He said he got more than he expected to.

> (**ELLA** *is a little proud of her son. She lights another cigarette.*)

ELLA. Tell him to hurry home.

FELICIA. Mamma said to hurry home. Okay. Bye.

> (**FELICIA** *hangs up the phone with a swift flip, then opens it again to start dialing another number.*)

He said he loves you.

> (*She puts the phone to her ear. She stands up while it rings, a bit nervous.*)

Hello? Dr. Marshall, it's Felicia Anderson. Yes, yes, I'm safe. At home with my mom, been here for the past two days. Is there someone at the museum? No, I haven't heard of anything happening, but I wanted to make sure the Allosaurus was going to be okay. You don't think anyone will try to break in and take parts of him, do you? I know he is mounted, but I *also* know that you guys are behind on your maintenance for the year and that the epoxy hasn't been retouched like it normally would be by now. The integrity of the bond holding the bones in place isn't nearly as strong as it normally is, which makes me concerned that someone with the proper tools and brute force could pry one of the vertebrae and the whole thing –

> (**FELICIA** *falls silent, listening intently.*)

Oh. Okay. But you do know that the response time will be delayed because of the riots, right? The grates are down, too? What about James, is he still there at night? He is? Okay. No, that's everything Dr. Marshall. You have a good night.

> (**FELICIA** *hangs up the phone.*)

Dr. Marshall said James is still reporting there at night. He's a good guard. Kept a kid last spring from prying out a T-Rex tooth.

ELLA. The Allosaurus is safe then? Good. Now we can all sleep better tonight.

FELICIA. I don't appreciate the sarcasm. It's not like we can just go find another one tomorrow.

> (**ELLA** *snuffs out her cigarette.*)

ELLA. I know, baby girl.

> (*She crosses to* **FELICIA**, *kissing her on the head.*)

That's what you are gonna do, remember? You are gonna find more of them big ole things.

FELICIA. You think so?

ELLA. Yes, my baby. And if your brother don't hurry up, you gonna have to dig him up, too.

FELICIA. He said he was running a bit slow. Didn't take the car.

ELLA. At least he did that much. Hell of a lot harder to be sneaking if you rollin' around in an Oldsmobile. Only good thing about havin' that car, ain't nobody gonna wanna steal it.

> (**FELICIA** *laughs a bit.*)

Have I told you how much I love that smile of yours?

(She kisses **FELICIA**'s *forehead again.)*

I'm gonna go look in the cabinets, see if we got a can of beans or somethin'. Make whatever he got us stretch a bit more. Put on one of my CDs, will ya? I wanna listen to somethin' else besides sirens all night.

*(***ELLA*** *exits toward the kitchen.* **FELICIA** *rummages around looking for the CDs.)*

FELICIA. I can't find the folder. Felix must have it in his room

ELLA. *(Offstage.)* Go look for it, would ya? I wanna hear somethin' grown and sexy.

*(***FELICIA*** *exits through the kitchen toward the bedrooms.)*

(The front door opens. In comes **FELIX**, *a slim and athletic black man. He has a large duffel bag full of food. As silently as he can, he sets the bag down.)*

(Offstage.) Felix? That you?

*(***FELIX*** *curses under his breath.)*

FELIX. Yeah, Ma. It's me.

ELLA. 'Bout damn time, son. I was getting worried about you.

*(***ELLA*** *enters and stands looking at him, faking disapproval.)*

Tell me you got us something good in all your foolishness.

FELIX. Mostly canned stuff, but enough to hold us through the week if we're smart about it.

ELLA. Now, you know your mamma don't condone stealin'.

(She looks in the bag.)

But you did what you had to do. So, I can't be too upset with ya. But now you ain't got no reason to go back out there, ya hear me?

*(***FELIX*** *heads for the door.)*

ELLA. What did I just say?

(**FELIX** *looks back at her, trying to hide his worry.*)

FELIX. I left something downstairs. Just gotta bring it up.

ELLA. Well, hurry up. I'm gonna get started on dinner, alright?

(**ELLA** *exits toward the kitchen.*)

(**FELIX** *stands at the door, looking out of it with regret.*)

FELIX. It's getting pretty bad out there, ya know. I passed by the Robinson's store. Still got black smoke seeping out of the windows a bit. Have you thought about us getting out of here, too? Just for a few days.

ELLA. *(Offstage.)* Boy, you know I can't leave my store. There ya go, talkin' out the side of your neck again.

FELIX. I'm just saying. If things get bad, we gotta plan for a way out.

(**ELLA** *enters the living room again. This time with an old apron tied around her waist. She puts her hands on her hips, one leg cocked out to the side. She becomes almost unmovable. Her voice is stern.*)

ELLA. I don't know what the hell has gotten into you, Felix. First, you are dumb enough to go out there with all them crazy-ass people. Don't get me wrong, the SPAM you grabbed is gonna give us somethin' to fill ourselves up with in the mornin', but you did that because you know we ain't going anywhere. So why even ask?

FELIX. I'm just asking you to consider it, okay? Things might get worse.

ELLA. Nothin' is gonna happen that hasn't already.

FELIX. Consider it.

(**ELLA** *stares at* **FELIX** *for a second before relaxing her posture some. She eventually nods.*)

ELLA. Hurry up and get whateva you've got down there. Check the back door on your way up.

FELIX. Where's Felicia?

ELLA. In your room looking for my CDs. Burn a copy if you want 'em so bad. If any of 'em start skippin', I'm crackin' your head.

> (**FELIX** *grins a bit. He calls out.*)

FELIX. Hey! Twin!

ELLA. What I tell you 'bout yellin' in my house! This ain't no zoo and you ain't a holla monkey.

> (**ELLA** *starts to exit. She calls out toward the bedrooms.*)

Felicia! Your brother wants you!

FELICIA. *(Calling back, offstage.)* I'm coming!

ELLA. What have I said about yellin' in my house!

> (**ELLA** *turns to* **FELIX.**)

Y'all ain't no good.

FELIX. Love you, too.

> (**ELLA** *exits, mumbling and chuckling under her breath.*)
>
> (**FELICIA** *enters.* **FELIX** *stops her before she can cross to him.*)

Close your eyes.

FELICIA. What are you doing?

FELIX. Twin. Close your eyes.

> (**FELICIA** *closes her eyes.*)

Put your hands out.

> *(She puts her hands out, in fists.)*

Open.

> *(He places something in her hands and closes her fingers around it. She opens her eyes, but before she can thank him in her excitement,*

> **FELIX** *puts a finger to his lips to keep her quiet.)*

FELIX. I wasn't able to grab a bunch of the candies to go inside. But, when this is all over, we'll go down to the 7-Eleven and take care of that. Hide it from Ma. She'll get pissed if she knows I had time to look for candy and didn't bring her any Lemonheads.

> *(**FELICIA** nods, large smile on her face. She starts talking loudly, loud enough for **ELLA** to hear.)*

FELICIA. Where did you put Mamma's Stevie Wonder CDs?

ELLA. *(Offstage.)* Did I say anything about Stevie, girl? Don't nobody wanna hear Stevie right now.

> *(**FELIX** and **FELICIA** laugh to themselves.)*

FELIX. Check by my boombox. On my desk. Her CD folder should be next to it.

> *(**FELICIA** laughs as she exits, playing with the gift Felix just gave her.)*

ELLA. *(Offstage.)* Don't nobody wanna hear Stevie!

> *(**FELIX** watches **FELICIA** exit. After a moment of silence, he moves over to the couch, moves the bags of clothes over to the recliner, and drapes them on the back of it. He pokes his head back into the kitchen. When he is convinced everyone is occupied, he quickly walks over to the front door. We hear some grunts and a few thumps from the hallway. **FELIX** enters again, dragging a white man in his thirties, **KELLY**. **KELLY** is sporting a bruise on the right side of his face. **FELIX** struggles to move him over to the couch, struggling to lift him on his own.)*

(Offstage.) What the hell you bringin' in?

FELIX. Just a sec, Ma!

(FELIX manages to get KELLY to the couch, attempting to sit him up but letting him flop over to one side. FELIX leaves him there, goes back out the door, and brings in a black backpack, setting it on the side of the couch. FELIX rushes back out the door.)

(FELICIA enters, holding the CD folder, flipping through the pages and not looking up. She stands behind the couch, unable to see KELLY on it.)

FELICIA. When did you get a copy of Christina? Did Mike burn it for you?

(FELICIA looks up, seeing FELIX isn't in the room. She moves around the room, toward the couch, head still buried in the CD folder. FELIX comes back in as FELICIA sees KELLY on the couch.)

(FELICIA starts to let out a scream, but FELIX rushes around and puts his hand on her mouth before she can get it all out.)

FELIX. Listen, listen... It's alright. I brought him up here, okay? Don't scream, okay?

(FELICIA nods her head. FELIX slowly removes his hand.)

He's knocked out right now. I wanna keep it that way. Until I know who he is.

FELICIA. You don't know who he is?

FELIX. No. Not yet. That's his bag. I haven't had a chance to go through it.

(FELIX takes the bag, sets it on the recliner, and opens it. He pushes stuff around in it for a moment, then something catches his attention. He quickly zips the bag back up.)

Those zip ties that you used last month for your build–

FELICIA. The Triceratops?

FELIX. Yeah, that model you built.

FELICIA. You aren't taking my Triceratops apart, are you? It took me forever to get that mounted.

FELIX. *(Snapping at her.)* Felicia! Please! Where are they?

> *(**FELICIA** is taken aback by **FELIX**'s tone.)*

I'm sorry, okay, but I need those zip ties.

FELICIA. Bottom shelf, end table next to my bed.

> *(**FELIX** exits toward the bedrooms. **FELICIA** looks at **KELLY** and then slowly unzips the bag. She rustles through it, her hand lingering on something in the bag. She pulls out a gun, standard-issue Glock, before pushing it deep into the bag and zipping it back up. **FELIX** enters, zip ties in hand, and heads over to **KELLY**. He turns him over, face in the cushions, and zip ties his hands together.)*

Who is he?

FELIX. I don't know.

FELICIA. What do you mean you don't know?

FELIX. I mean what I said. I don't know, okay?

FELICIA. But he has a gun.

FELIX. Did you open the bag?

FELICIA. He has a gun, Felix.

FELIX. Did you open the bag? Why did you open the bag?

FELICIA. What does it matter if I opened the bag? Obviously I opened the bag. I don't have x-ray vision. And I can't read minds either, so you are gonna have to tell me why there is a man with a gun in our house.

FELIX. Hush up! What if Ma hears?

FELICIA. She's gonna notice a white man on her couch eventually, Felix. You don't think there are gonna be questions when she does?

FELIX. Whatever they are, they won't be why the man has a gun.

(**FELIX** *walks over to the bag, unzips it, and starts looking for the gun.*)

Where is it?

FELICIA. At the bottom of the bag. I put it down there.

FELIX. You touched it?

(**FELIX** *grabs the gun, wrapping it in the bottom of his shirt, rubbing it between his hands to clean it.*)

(**FELIX** *goes over to the back of the chair, rips off a piece of plastic wrapped around the clothes, and wraps the gun in it. He slides the gun under the chair.*)

You're supposed to be the smart one, and you're touching guns from people you don't even know.

FELICIA. Who is he? Why is he in here?

FELIX. I had to bring him, okay?

FELICIA. Had to? You had to drag a man up the stairs into our apartment? With a gun?

FELIX. Can you stop with the gun? I had to bring him because I hit him. I hit him and knocked him out.

FELICIA. You... You what?

FELIX. I knocked him out. He came up on me and I hit him.

(**FELICIA** *crosses over to* **KELLY**. *She notices the bruise on the side of his face.*)

FELICIA. Jesus.

FELIX. Jesus ain't got nothin' to do with this.

FELICIA. What you gonna tell Mamma?

FELIX. I haven't thought that far yet.

FELICIA. You don't know who he is, what you gonna tell Mamma –

FELIX. I know, I know. Jesus, Felicia!

FELICIA. Jesus ain't got nothin' to do with this, remember?

(**KELLY** *lets out a groan.*)

He's waking up.

(**ELLA** *calls out.*)

ELLA. *(Offstage.)* I don't hear no music, baby girl! Dinner is almost ready.

>(**FELIX** *goes over to* **KELLY**, *peering over him to see if his eyes are open.*)

FELIX. He's still out. I'm not sure how long. We gotta do somethin'.

FELICIA. We? I don't gotta do anything. This is all on you.

ELLA. *(Offstage.)* My music, baby girl!

FELIX. Put on somethin' before she come in here wonderin'.

>(**FELICIA** *grabs the CD folder and fumbles through it quickly. She grabs a CD and puts it in the CD player. Old school R&B fills the room. She starts to walk back toward the couch.*)

>(**ELLA** *walks in briskly, heading straight for the radio. She turns up the music. She turns back to head into the kitchen, not looking at the couch. She doesn't even look at her children.*)

ELLA. Come give me a hand, baby girl. I want you to pull the green beans while I fry up the SPAM.

>(**ELLA** *exits before* **FELIX** *and* **FELICIA** *can say anything to her.*)

>(**KELLY** *groans again, obviously waking up this time.* **FELIX** *waves* **FELICIA** *on toward the kitchen.*)

FELIX. Stall.

>(**FELICIA** *tuns offstage toward the kitchen.* **KELLY** *starts to open his eyes, wincing from pain as he moves.*)

>(**FELIX** *sits on the couch next to him, helping sit him up.*)

Hey...hey. Listen. Who are you?

(**KELLY** *tries to move his arms but can't. His eyes get wide. He starts to struggle.*)

KELLY. What the hell?

(**FELIX** *motions for him to keep quiet.*)

FELIX. Calm down. Just... / Calm down.

KELLY. Where the hell am I?

(**KELLY** *tries to stand up.* **FELIX** *pushes him back down.*)

FELIX. Calm the hell down, alright?

(**KELLY** *starts to thrash about. Yelling the whole time.*)

KELLY. Let me go! Let me go, you bastard!

(**KELLY** *starts kicking at* **FELIX**.)

(**ELLA** *comes rushing in, seeing* **KELLY** *kicking and screaming.*)

ELLA. What the hell is going on?

(**ELLA** *turns off the CD player.* **FELIX** *gets on top of* **KELLY**'s *feet.* **KELLY** *connects with* **FELIX**'s *side.*)

KELLY. Let me go!

FELIX. Hand me a shirt.

ELLA. Who the hell is he?

FELIX. Hand me a shirt!

(**ELLA** *pulls a shirt from a dry-cleaning bag, tossing it at* **FELIX**. *He uses the shirt to tie up* **KELLY**'s *feet.*)

(**KELLY** *falls quiet for a moment.*)

KELLY. Trash can. I'm gonna puke.

FELIX. Felicia! Grab me the trash can from the bathroom!

(**FELIX** *turns to* **ELLA**.)

He was out there, Ma. He was outside.

ELLA. Don't mean you had to bring him inside.

FELIX. I didn't have no choice.

> (**FELICIA** *enters with a small trash can.* **FELIX** *places it in front of* **KELLY**, *who turns and hurls into it, his energy leaving him each time he vomits.*)

FELICIA. IS he okay?

FELIX. Forget him. He got me pretty good.

ELLA. You gonna have to worry about a hell of a lot more if you don't tell me what is going on.

FELIX. You gotta promise not to get / too upset.

ELLA. I ain't gonna promise a damn thing. You tell me why this man is in my house right now.

FELIX. Twin, go get a glass of water for him, will ya?

> (**FELICIA** *hesitates, then exits.*)

Look, it all just happened kinda fast, alright? And you said so yourself, those people out there are crazy.

ELLA. You haven't answered my question. Why the hell is he here?

FELIX. I knocked him out right outside the store.

> (**KELLY** *wretches again, dry heaving.*)

ELLA. Good job, you knocked out a drunk. I can smell the bourbon from here.

FELIX. He was tryin' to mug me, Ma.

ELLA. Oh, so now he's a mugger.

FELIX. No, Ma, listen.

> (**FELICIA** *enters with a glass of water. She sits on the couch next to* **KELLY**.)

ELLA. I'm done listening. You hit the man, good job for protecting yourself. But that don't mean a damn thing. You don't know this man from Adam.

FELIX. What would Dad have done?

ELLA. See, that kinda foolishness is exactly what I don't wanna hear. Your dad ain't here. I am.

FELIX. I can't just leave that man out there, Ma. He could barely stand up when he grabbed me.

ELLA. That ain't your problem. You didn't make the fool get drunk.

FELIX. Imagine what would have happened if they would have caught him out there. I hit him 'cause he grabbed me. Others wouldn't need that much of a reason.

ELLA. You just like your father, and right now, that ain't no good thing.

>   (**ELLA** *crosses over to the couch.*)

How's he doing?

FELICIA. Sleep again.

ELLA. I want you to listen to me. Both of ya. This man... find out who he is. You're a fool, Felix. And I take it you knew he was here, Felicia?

>   (**FELICIA** *nods.*)

FELIX. I was gonna tell you once I had everything figured out.

ELLA. Well we in it now. *We.* And I hate to admit it, but we can't just toss him back out there. Not till mornin'.

>   (**ELLA** *starts to exit toward the kitchen, furious.*)

Felicia, clear the table. Your canned meat's gonna get cold.

>   (**FELICIA** *leaves* **KELLY**'s *side and starts clearing the books and papers off of the table.*)

Find out who he is.

>   (**ELLA** *exits.*)

>   (**FELICIA** *stares at* **FELIX** *for a moment.*)

FELICIA. Why did you bring up Dad?

FELIX. I wasn't wrong.

FELICIA. That's not the point.

FELIX. Don't you start on me, too, alright?

FELICIA. She doesn't like when you bring him up.
FELIX. Would he have helped him, yes or no?
FELICIA. Well, yeah.
FELIX. Then that's all I care about.

>*(**FELIX** grabs the trash can and starts to exit.)*

Let me know if he starts to wake up again.

>*(**FELIX** exits. **FELICIA** watches him leave. Red and blue lights speed by the window, sirens are heard.)*
>
>*(Lights down.)*

Scene Two

*(Lights up on the family sitting down at the table, eating, while music softly plays from the CD player. In front of the couch, where **KELLY** still lies, sits a plate of food. A gunshot rings out, along with the sound of distant glass breaking.)*

*(**KELLY** groans on the couch and starts to move. **FELIX** goes to the couch and helps sit him up. **ELLA** grabs her plate, not finished, along with **FELIX**'s plate, and takes them to the kitchen. **FELICIA** doesn't move.)*

FELIX. Here.

*(**FELIX** places the water to **KELLY**'s lips, helping him drink.)*

Now don't go freakin' out. We don't want what happened last time to happen again.

*(**KELLY** nods.)*

You must of wrestled with that bottle pretty good before you ran into me.

KELLY. Didn't expect a punch like that to come from a kid like you.

FELIX. I was wonderin' if you remembered that.

KELLY. My face won't let me forget.

FELICIA. I'll get some ice.

*(**FELICIA** stands, picking up her plate, and exits toward the kitchen.)*

FELIX. Look, I'ma be straight with you. I don't know what you were doin' out there or why you were following me, but you're safe right now.

KELLY. I can take care of myself.

FELIX. Think what you want, but you ain't a-hundred percent right now. And, if we don't do somethin' about your face, it's gonna swell up like a pumpkin.

KELLY. If you untie me, I'll be just fine. I don't have time for this right now, okay? I have to get home.

> (**FELICIA** *enters, holding a bag of ice wrapped in a towel.*)

FELICIA. You can't go back out there. Curfew was at six. Things are pretty bad out there I imagine. We heard some shots earlier. People getting more worked up.

> (*She places the towel to his face.*)

Too cold?

KELLY. It's fine.

FELICIA. Good. Are you hungry? Felix could hold this while I feed you.

KELLY. I could hold it myself if my hands were free.

FELIX. Not yet. I have some questions for you.

KELLY. What is this?

FELIX. It's nothin' but me trying to figure out the best way to get you home, alright? After you kicked me I don't really trust you with any loose limbs so excuse me if I'm / – I wouldn't have hit you if you hadn't touched me.

KELLY. You hit me first, and I don't even know where the hell I am.

FELICIA. You're in our apartment, above Starlight Cleaners on the corner of Vine and 13th. Right next to that sandwich shop that sells the fresh-squeezed lemonade too.

FELIX. What are you doin'?

FELICIA. He said he doesn't know where he is. I'm tellin' him.

KELLY. Look, that's not what I meant –

FELICIA. I'm Felicia Anderson. This is my twin brother, Felix. My mamma, Ella Robins, she's in the other room. She ain't too happy with Felix at the moment. But she'll get over it. She always does.

FELIX. You think tellin' this man our names is a smart idea?

FELICIA. When he eventually leaves, he was gonna see where he was anyway. What harm will it do now?

(Silence settles between them. **KELLY** *groans in pain.)*

KELLY. You got any Aspirin?

FELICIA. Felix will get it for you.

> *(**FELICIA** eyes **FELIX**, motioning for him to go to the kitchen.)*
>
> *(**FELIX** exits.)*

My brother means well. Always has. Just can't seem to get it right all the time. Don't know what it is about him, but he has to help. I say it's the part of my daddy that stuck around, but Mamma don't like that much.

KELLY. Look...uh...

FELICIA. Felicia.

KELLY. Can you shut up for a minute? My head is already hurting.

> *(**FELICIA** falls silent. She removes the bag of ice from his face, setting it next to him. She grabs a dinosaur book and sits in the Lay-Z-Boy chair, beginning to read.)*
>
> *(**KELLY** struggles to find a way to get the bag to his face.)*

When are you going to free my hands?

> *(Silence.)*

Listen, do you know how much trouble you'll be in if... when I get out of here? You and your thieving brother –

FELICIA. *(Not looking up from her book.)* He took what he had to for us.

KELLY. That's the kind of thinking that gets people in deep shit.

FELICIA. *(Calling out to **FELIX**.)* Never mind, twin! I think we'll be fine without Aspirin.

KELLY. Are you serious?

> *(**FELICIA** doesn't say a word. She closes her current book, gets another, goes back to the chair, and continues to read.)*

(**FELIX** *enters on the tense scene. Aspirin in hand, he walks over to* **KELLY**. *He holds out his hand, offering to give him the Aspirin.* **KELLY** *takes one pill in his mouth before spitting it out across the room.*)

FELICIA. I told you we'd be fine without.

KELLY. I'm gonna tell you again, you need to let me go.

(*A siren passes by. Voices outside get louder.*)

FELIX. If this is about you gettin' home, maybe we can get a call out. Let 'em know you're okay. Alright? But I'm not gonna let you go back out there and get yourself killed.

KELLY. There are few options in this situation. Only one of them ends well for you. Uncut my hands, give me my bag, and I'll be just fine on my own.

FELICIA. Let him go.

FELIX. With all that's goin' on outside.

(*Flash of red and yellow as a fire erupts a few streets over, lighting up the sky outside the window.*)

FELICIA. Mamma would agree with me. She don't want him here in the first place. Now he don't wanna be here? Let him go.

(**FELICIA** *grabs the plate of food from the table, exiting toward the kitchen.*)

FELIX. You ain't doin' yourself any favors by headin' back out there. You got a car?

KELLY. It's not important.

FELIX. You ain't gonna get no closer to home with folks actin' the way they are.

(**ELLA** *enters. Scissors in hand.*)

ELLA. Let him join 'em if he wants.

(**ELLA** *extends the scissors to* **FELIX**. **FELIX** *hesitates.*)

Boy, move.

(**ELLA** *crosses over to* **KELLY**, *cuts his hands free, and walks away.*)

(**ELLA** *pulls* **FELIX** *close.*)

You can't save everyone, aight? Neither could your father. Make sure the man has his things. Lock the door after him.

(*She kisses his forehead, crossing to the kitchen table and lighting a cigarette.*)

(**FELIX** *is motionless for a second.*)

KELLY. You should listen to your mamma. Can't save everyone.

FELIX. There's your bag. I'll be waitin' downstairs.

(**FELIX** *exits through the front door, slamming it.*)

(**ELLA** *takes a long drag.*)

KELLY. Filthy habit.

ELLA. So is too much whiskey.

(*She lets the smoke billow out.*)

KELLY. What time is it?

ELLA. Time you got goin'.

KELLY. I'm just askin' what the time was.

(**ELLA** *puts her cigarette down.*)

ELLA. I don't know if you noticed, but I ain't rather hospitable right now. Normally I would walk you down the stairs, me holdin' your bag and your plate wrapped up in foil to take home.

But between you kickin' my son, tellin' my daughter to shut up, and refusin' the generosity I managed to pull out of my ass for you… I'd say you've extended your welcome here at Starlight Cleaners. Felix is waitin' for you downstairs. He'll show you out and point you in any direction you wanna go, as long as it's away from here.

(**ELLA** *picks up her cigarette.*)

ELLA. You got a complaint, you can file it downstairs.

> (**ELLA** *exits toward the kitchen.*)
>
> (**KELLY** *reaches for his bag, searching through it. He notices the gun is missing. He starts searching under the cushions and on his person. He looks on the kitchen table and in the chair. Everywhere but under the chair.*)

KELLY. Shit.

> (**KELLY** *goes through his bag again, frantically.*)

Shit shit shit shit!

> (**ELLA** *comes back in the room.*)

ELLA. You ain't left yet?

KELLY. Where is it?

ELLA. The door ain't moved.

KELLY. Where is it? Where did you put it?

ELLA. I don't know what the hell you're talkin' about.

KELLY. I wasn't going to do anything when I leave, but if I don't get it back, I'm not gonna have much choice.

ELLA. You better calm down. I don't know what you / are talking about.

KELLY. My gun! Where the hell is my gun?

> (**ELLA** *stares at him.*)
>
> (*Beat.*)

ELLA. Felicia! Get your ass in here!

> (*Suddenly, there is a loud bang heard outside of the window, followed by a surge of voices. Yelling, screaming. The sound of breaking glass rings through the air. Loud noises are heard from downstairs.*)

KELLY. What the hell was that?

> (**ELLA** *runs to the window.*)

ELLA. They're breakin' in the store! Shit. Felix!

(FELICIA runs in.)

FELICIA. Mamma! / Where's Felix.

KELLY. Help me find it / and I can help.

ELLA. Calm down baby girl, okay? Get in your room and shut the door.

FELICIA. I'm scared, Mamma.

KELLY. Where did you put it? / Where did you put my gun?

ELLA. Tell me about it after all this, baby girl. / Get yourself locked up and don't come out till I tell ya.

KELLY. Jesus, people. I'm tryin' to help you.

ELLA. Then shut up for a second. Baby girl. Go.

(FELICIA exits toward the bedrooms.)

(ELLA rushes over to the closet and pulls out a baseball bat.)

You wanna help? Go get my son.

(The sound of quick footsteps coming to the front door are heard. KELLY grabs the baseball bat from ELLA, crosses to the door, and takes an attack stance.)

(FELIX flings the door open. Slamming it shut. He rushes over to the sofa and starts to push it.)

FELIX. Help me!

(ELLA goes to her son and starts to move the couch. Voices are heard in the hall outside of the door. KELLY drops the bat and helps to push the couch the rest of the way to the door. They stand it on its end, pressed against the door, right as there is a loud bang from the other side.)

(ELLA starts to silently pray. She grabs her son's hand.)

KELLY. Fuck.

> (**KELLY** *runs offstage. Once offstage, a gut-wrenching sound is heard. More throw up.*)

ELLA. Go check on your sister. In her room.

FELIX. You okay?

> (**ELLA** *nods, eyes still closed in prayer.*)

ELLA. Lord Jesus.

> (**ELLA** *walks over and grabs her cigarette. She lights it and takes a long draw. Another bang is heard from the other side of the door, voices still echoing up the stairwell.*)

> (**KELLY** *enters, cleaning throw up from the edges of his mouth. He walks over to the window, leaning against it, tired, cringing.*)

KELLY. Terrible time for a hangover.

ELLA. Never heard of a good time for one.

> (**KELLY** *sits down at the table.*)

You ain't goin' out there. Not with all them folks down there.

KELLY. I figured as much. I'm fine with that. But I need my gun.

ELLA. I don't know nothin' about your gun.

> (*The sound of more breaking glass.*)

Lord, they better not break my conveyor. Just got that sucka fixed.

> (**FELIX** *enters, crossing to* **ELLA**.)

FELIX. She's alright. A little shaken. Told her to lie down for a bit.

ELLA. How many of those fools were down there?

FELIX. I dunno.

> (*Nods toward* **KELLY**.)

ELLA. You take somethin' that's his?

(**FELIX** *glances over to* **KELLY**. *He doesn't answer.*)

What you have of his, son? He says you have his gun.

FELIX. Ma, listen –

ELLA. Yes or no.

(**FELIX** *still doesn't answer.*)

You talked me into keepin' him here and now you go mute. Did you take his gun or / not?

FELIX. Yes.

ELLA. *(To* **KELLY***)* There. Now you can let me smoke without askin' me questions.

KELLY. Where is it?

FELIX. Hidden.

KELLY. Where is it?

FELIX. You walkin' the streets and you totin' a gun around, stoppin' people for what? / 'Cause you think you can?

KELLY. The gun. Where did you put it?

ELLA. Give him the damn gun.

FELIX. Why? So he can stop someone else and shoot 'em? Givin' an aggressive man / a weapon in a riot just seems dumb.

KELLY. Aggressive?

FELIX. I'm not giving you the gun. Not until we can get you out of here. So just...just wait.

KELLY. You don't understand what you're doing. You don't know what the hell is going on! I have to get out of here, okay?

FELIX. You're not goin' anywhere!

KELLY. I have to go!

FELIX. No!

(**FELIX** *and* **KELLY** *stare at each other.*)

KELLY. You can and will be brought up on charges for stealing an officer's firearm as well as holding him hostage.

FELIX. What the hell are you talkin' about?

KELLY. You wanna know my name? I'm officer Kelly Holton, Cincinnati PD.

FELIX. Shit.

ELLA. Jesus Christ. A cop?

FELIX. Ma, I didn't know.

(**ELLA** *crosses to* **FELIX**.)

ELLA. A cop?

KELLY. Tell me where the damn gun is.

FELIX. How do we know he's tellin' the truth?

KELLY. Don't be stupid, alright?

FELIX. Cops don't stumble the streets drunk!

KELLY. What do you want? My badge number?

FELIX. That proves nothin'.

ELLA. Felix!

FELIX. Ma, this man can't be tellin' the truth.

ELLA. And what if he is? You gonna keep a gun from a cop? Do you know the amount of trouble you can get in? We can get in?

FELIX. Then why isn't he out there?

KELLY. It's called a shift. Mine was done. Look, you don't believe me, that's fine. Give me your phone, I'll make a call.

FELIX. To hell you will!

ELLA. Felix! Go check on your sister.

(**FELIX** *doesn't move.*)

I don't know what in God's name has taken hold of you, but I know that you better back down before he watches you get beat down right here, right now. You got five seconds to take your narrow behind in there and check on your sister.

(**FELIX** *still doesn't move.*)

Boy!

FELIX. Fine.

ELLA. Give him your phone.

> (**FELIX** *looks at* **ELLA**. *She puts her hand out.* **FELIX** *pulls his cell phone out of his pocket, hands it to* **ELLA**, *then exits toward the bedrooms.*)

KELLY. Hard-headed.

ELLA. He prefers steadfast.

> (**ELLA** *hands* **KELLY** *the phone. He looks at the phone. He starts to dial.*)

Police aren't about to bust in here after this, are they?

KELLY. I'm not calling the cops.

ELLA. What?

KELLY. Shit. No service.

ELLA. Who you callin'?

KELLY. You want proof, don't you? Let me get my proof.

> (**KELLY** *tries to call again. Fails.*)

Shit. Shit shit shit.

ELLA. Extensive vocabulary. Impressive.

> (**KELLY** *looks at her, shocked she would make jokes.*)

> (**FELICIA** *comes rushing into the room. She rushes to* **ELLA**, *wrapping her arms around her.* **FELIX** *walks into the room.*)

FELIX. She didn't wanna stay in there anymore.

FELICIA. Mamma!

ELLA. Baby girl. It's okay. Shhh. Don't worry. They ain't gonna get up here.

> (*She nods at* **KELLY**.)

How long before people can get this mess under control? Don't you get calls about this sorta stuff?

KELLY. Someone has to report it.

> (**KELLY** *tosses the phone back to* **FELIX**. *He catches it.*)

KELLY. Kinda stuck if we can't get a call out.

FELIX. Still no proof, huh?

ELLA. Drop it, alright? Officer Holton –

FELICIA. Officer?

> (**FELICIA** *pokes her head up. She looks at* **KELLY** *for a second. She starts to shake a bit, nervousness getting the best of her.*)

ELLA. Baby girl, look at me. Look at me.

FELICIA. (*Speaking swiftly, her eyes closed. Mumbling.*) The average length of the Velociraptor was between five to six feet. Named by Henry F. Osborn / in 1924 the name means the speedy thief. The first fossils were found in Mongolia and the animal is one of the most famous meat-eating dinosaurs.

ELLA. Not now baby girl. Come on. / Felix.

KELLY. What's happening?

> (**FELIX** *crosses over to* **FELICIA**.)

FELIX. She gets like this when she's nervous. Twin. Hey, Twin. Listen to me. We can't go backwards right now. Okay? You've been doing so well. We need you to stay with us. Stay with us right now.

FELICIA. The Velociraptor has a sharp and retractable three-and-a-half inch claw on each foot. They are believed to be able to run up to forty miles per hour when need be and they hunted in packs.

> (**FELICIA** *continues to mumble to herself random facts.*)

KELLY. What's wrong?

ELLA. She's on the spectrum.

> (**ELLA** *grabs a dinosaur book.*)

She goes back to what she's comfortable with.

FELIX. Hey twin. Come sit with me. Can you sit with me? Yeah?

KELLY. If I could get my gun, I could get out of your way.

ELLA. You wanna be out of the way? Sit down.

>   (**FELIX** *and* **FELICIA** *sit at the table.* **ELLA** *opens the book in front of* **FELICIA**. **KELLY** *crosses to* **FELIX**.)

KELLY. Give me the gun.

>   (**FELIX** *ignores* **KELLY**, *is going through the book with* **FELICIA**.)

Give me the gun. Where the fuck is the goddamn gun!

>   (**FELICIA** *starts to rattle off random facts, louder this time, her eyes closed tightly.*)
>
>   (**ELLA** *takes a seat at the table, putting her arm around* **FELICIA** *and pulling her in tightly, trying to calm her down.*)
>
>   (**FELIX** *jumps up, getting into* **KELLY**'s *face.*)

FELIX. She said to sit down, damn it! You can't give us one damn moment?

KELLY. I want to leave!

FELIX. Then wait!

>   (**FELIX** *stares at* **KELLY**. *Eventually,* **KELLY** *crosses over to the recliner.*)
>
>   (**FELIX** *tosses* **KELLY** *the phone.*)

Get me someone who can tell me who you are, and I'll give you your damn gun.

>   (**FELIX** *crosses over to the table again. He huddles in with* **FELICIA** *and* **ELLA**. **KELLY** *dials the phone again. Nothing.*)

KELLY. Fuck.

>   (*Lights begin to fade, the colors of the riots pouring through the window.*)

Scene Three

(Lights come up, dimly, as **KELLY** *is pacing back and forth, phone still glued to his hands.* **FELIX** *sits at the kitchen table, watching him. Outside it is not as loud, but unified chanting is heard. The lights through the window are subdued, but sirens are still heard in the background as they speed around the city a few blocks away.)*

FELIX. You gonna wear out the carpet.

*(****KELLY**** ignores him.)*

Will you sit down for a bit? You're makin' me nervous.

KELLY. I'm making you nervous? I'm stuck here and I'm making you nervous.

FELIX. I'm sure you can leave now. No one's downstairs no more.

KELLY. I'm not leaving without –

FELIX. Without the gun. I get it. Jesus, man. You would think I'd taken your kidney or somethin'.

KELLY. I need it.

FELIX. You can't prove that. You haven't gotten through a single time to whoever it is you're tryin' to call and it has been almost two hours. You pacing like that ain't gonna clear up the lines. Only time will. So, I'm askin' you to sit down, please.

*(****KELLY**** looks at* **FELIX** *for a moment. He closes the phone and sits on the couch, which is still against the door. He is silent for a second before he starts to ask a question, then decides not to.)*

FELIX. Mind if I ask for my phone back?

KELLY. Why?

FELIX. The battery on that thing is pretty much shit. Doesn't last more than an afternoon, and really, you callin' on it didn't do it any favors. I'm going to charge it.

(**KELLY** *eyes* **FELIX**.)

God, man. Fine.
(Calling out.) Twin! Can you bring me a cell phone charger?
(To **KELLY**.*)* I'll charge it in here, okay?

KELLY. Good.

FELIX. I swear man...

(**FELIX** *turns on the radio, soft jazz music flooding into the room again.*)

KELLY. Mind if we listen to something else?

FELIX. You don't like jazz?

KELLY. Not particularly...

FELIX. What kinda stuff you listen to? Lemme guess...you listen to those Coldplay guys, don't you? Naw, that's too laid-back for some guy like you. You look more like a Linkin Park kinda dude. Something a bit more harsh and angry.

(**KELLY** *starts to laugh to himself.*)

KELLY. This is dumb.

FELIX. What's dumb about it? I'm just tryin' to get to know you.

(**FELICIA** *enters, charger in hand.*)

Twin, what kind of music you think the man listens to?

FELICIA. Does it matter?

(He looks at **FELICIA**, *then back to* **KELLY**.*)*

FELIX. No. I guess it doesn't.

(**FELIX** *takes the charger from* **FELICIA**, *plugs it and the phone in.*)

There. Charging. You can turn the radio to whatever you want.

(**FELIX** *exits.*)

(**FELICIA** *stands, arms crossed, looking at* **KELLY**. **KELLY** *crosses from the couch and sits* *at the table, tuning the radio. As he scans through stations, he eventually stops when he hears the voice of a* **REPORTER.**)

REPORTER. *(Voice-over.)* – Halfway across the city. As the community continues to react to the acquittal of Patrolman Stephen Roach in the death of nineteen-year-old African-American, Timothy Thomas. While Roach is on leave from the force, many are asking for the names of the other officers involved, citing a need for all nine of those involved to apologize to the community. All attempts to obtain a statement from the police have proved fruitless, as the riot stretches on and the number of injuries and arrests climb. This is Ronald Hender –

(**KELLY** *switches the radio off. He is silent for a second, thinking.*)

FELICIA. Sad stuff, all this. Isn't it?

KELLY. Yeah.

FELICIA. I saw the pictures from the police station. How they hung the flag upside down and smashed the windows and everything...were you there?

KELLY. No. I wasn't.

FELICIA. Oh.

(Pause.)

KELLY. Can I... Can I apologize for earlier? I mean... That's not me. Not really.

FELICIA. Okay.

KELLY. What do you mean, okay?

FELICIA. Mamma says that forgiving too quickly ain't always the smartest thing to do. So, I usually don't. Takes time to see if someone really means it or not.

KELLY. I can see that. I mean, I get it.

FELICIA. Only person I can forgive quickly is Felix. He always use to apologize for everything. Even when he didn't do it. For a while he would say he was sorry every day. I'd ask him what for but he never really told me.

But, when I said I forgave him, he always smiled after. So I always did.

> *(Pause.)*

KELLY. So, can I ask what's with the dinosaurs?

> *(**FELICIA** lights up.)*

FELICIA. Oh! Yeah! Ummm...

> *(She looks around for her big dinosaur book, grabs it, and sets it in front of **KELLY**. She doesn't sit down with him. Instead, she begins to walk around the room with this excited and kinetic energy.)*

These things are the building blocks, the ancestors for millions of species.

Mammals aside. But the world is populated with so many more birds and lizards and amphibians than there are mammals. And these were the pinnacle of it all. Massive creatures taller than this here building and then they are all gone.

> *(She stares at **KELLY**, who returns her look with a blank one.)*

Turn to page one-seven-five.

> *(**KELLY** flips through the book.)*

You see that up there? That was found in Berlin. You know what it is?

> *(**KELLY** shakes his head.)*

They call it the Urvogel and it was considered the first bird. It goes back over 150 million years ago. It's gone, yes, but there are tons of other birds still here. But they came from that.

KELLY. I don't... It's just a bunch of dead things.

FELICIA. True. But that's where it gets interesting. Dead things tell stories, too. Well, not really, but the way they died can tell us a lot.

> *(**FELICIA** sits at the table, leaning in to **KELLY**.)*

FELICIA. Can you keep a secret? Well, it's not really a secret, but it hasn't been published or proved or anything, so in scientific terms it's still a secret. I'm working it out with Dr. Marshall at the museum, but we submitted a preliminary theory with my graduate school application, and I hope that they don't think I'm just –

> (**KELLY** *reaches for her hand.*)

KELLY. *(Gently.)* Calm down and tell me.

> (**FELICIA** *pulls her hand back.*)

FELICIA. I don't like that. I don't like when people I don't know touch me.

KELLY. Okay, okay. Just... What's your theory?

> (**FELICIA** *stands and collects herself a bit, back to* **KELLY.** *She closes her eyes and takes a deep breath before continuing.*)

FELICIA. Right...umm...my theory.

> (**ELLA** *enters, standing by the exit to the kitchen. She watches from there.*)
>
> (**ELLA** *closes her eyes, almost as if she is reciting the following.*)

There have already been five major extinction events. The last was the one that is credited with the elimination of the dinosaurs. Between all of them they have one thing in common, and that is that it was unstoppable.

> (**FELICIA** *relaxes a bit.*)

One. Drop in sea levels. Two. Global cooling. Three. Comet, volcanoes, or a combination of the two – not really sure. Four. Floods of lava. Five. Several mile wide asteroids. All of them, destructive and unstoppable. And it's going to happen again.

KELLY. Positive outlook.

FELICIA. No, it's not like that. I mean...

> (**FELICIA** *turns around to face* **KELLY** *and notices* **ELLA.***)

ELLA. Go ahead, baby girl. Finish. Just like you practiced.

FELICIA. Okay. Umm… Taking into account the rate of deforestation and the number of animals that have gone extinct in the last three hundred years, we can theorize that we are at the beginning of one. The sixth great mass extinction. Only, this time it's different. This time we see it coming and we know what the cause is. It's us. You and me and even Mamma.

ELLA. I don't have no part in that.

> (**ELLA** *smiles.*)

FELICIA. Okay. Not Mamma.

KELLY. Like the dodo bird was hunted to extinction.

ELLA. *(With a laugh.)* Look at you, all knowledgeable and shit.

FELICIA. Exactly. Except…bigger. And maybe some of the answers as to how we save those things is in understanding what we lost when we lost the dinosaurs.

ELLA. Baby girl is gonna be one of those bone scientists. Tell us what we don't know about 'em.

FELICIA. It's just a theory though. I have to work out the gaps in it. Dr. Marshall says it's on the right track. You know, just last week, we were sittin' in his office and he told me –

ELLA. Baby girl.

FELICIA. Yes, Mamma?

ELLA. I know you haven't been 'round too many people with hangovers, but yammerin' on and on don't cure it for him

> (*To* **KELLY**.)

You think you could eat now?

KELLY. Would you hate me if I said I wasn't a SPAM fan?

ELLA. I'd say you might have to get over that tonight.

KELLY. That's fine.

ELLA. Go pop his plate in the microwave. I put it in the fridge earlier.

(**FELICIA** *exits into the kitchen.*)

ELLA. You got a kid, don't you. Young one.

KELLY. Huh?

ELLA. Most people don't listen to rambling like that. Not without practice.

KELLY. He's nine.

ELLA. Can I tell you that pisses me off a bit? You being out there and you have a kid at home waiting for you.

KELLY. He isn't there. Doesn't live with me.

ELLA. My apologies.

KELLY. No need.

ELLA. No luck I take it reachin' someone?

KELLY. Not yet.

ELLA. Mind helpin' me move the couch?

(**ELLA** *and* **KELLY** *move the couch back, removing it from in front of the door.* **ELLA** *starts for the door.*)

KELLY. What are you doing?

ELLA. Gotta check to see how bad it is. File insurance in the mornin'.

KELLY. It's still not safe. Where's that bat?

(**ELLA** *grabs the bat, handing it to* **KELLY**.)

ELLA. Back left corner, past the big rack, you'll see the main conveyor. Check that first. Then the steamer.

KELLY. What's that look like?

ELLA. Hold on.

(*Calling out.*)

Felix! Come here!

(*To* **KELLY**.)

I'm gonna send him with you, alright?

KELLY. Your son doesn't really have the highest regard for me.

ELLA. Tough shit for him, isn't it?

(**FELIX** *enters.*)

Head down with Kelly, check out what's what. And before you say a word, I don't care. He offered, I'm tellin' you to go, so that's that.

(**FELIX** *looks at her, at* **KELLY**, *walks right past them both, reaches into the closet, grabs a flashlight, and heads out of the house.*)

He'll be alright. He gets uptight, just like his daddy. Just holla back up at me if he gives you too much attitude.

(**ELLA** *reaches into the closet, hands a flashlight to* **KELLY**. **KELLY** *takes the flashlight and exits.*)

(*Lights fade.*)

Scene Four

*(Lights up in front of the apartment set, detached from the home. **FELIX** stands there, flashlight in hand, searching through the darkness of the cleaners below. The sounds of the chanting are noticeably louder now. **KELLY** comes in after him, flashlight shining around the space.)*

KELLY. I'll admit, quite a set-up you guys got here.

FELIX. Yeah. Are we looking for anything specific?

KELLY. Main conveyor then the steamer?

FELIX. Stay here. Watch for broken glass.

*(**FELIX** walks to the other side of the stage. He starts examining the conveyor just out of sight of the audience.)*

KELLY. Is there a light somewhere?

FELIX. And let everyone know we're down here? There's still people outside.

KELLY. But I have the bat.

FELIX. Don't forget I took you out.

KELLY. I was drunk. Hardly counts.

FELIX. That what you gonna tell your cop buddies when you turn me in?

KELLY. What makes you think I'm gonna turn you in?

FELIX. Never in the history of ever has a black man hit a cop and gotten away with it.

KELLY. You believe I'm a cop then.

FELIX. I believe you're more than you seem. Not sure what that more is yet.

KELLY. Then can we cut the crap between us?

FELIX. I never said I trusted you.

KELLY. Your mom does.

FELIX. We ain't the same person.

*(**FELIX** kneels down.)*

Shit.

KELLY. What?

FELIX. Some asshole decided they needed to rip the whole panel off the damn thing.

KELLY. What does someone want with that?

FELIX. Why don't you ask them? I'm sure they're still out there. Everything else seems alright, but that doesn't do us any good if we can't turn the damn thing on.

(**KELLY** *starts to walk over to* **FELIX**.)

KELLY. How's it work?

FELIX. The panel sits here. You hang the clothes up here and when a customer comes in to pick up their stuff you press a button, movin' it left and right.

KELLY. Gonna stop you guys from working?

FELIX. Naww. Broken windows might, though. I'm gonna go check the steamer.

(**FELIX** *exits.*)

(**KELLY** *stares at the conveyor for a moment before crossing back across the space. The chanting outside is heard clearly.*)

KELLY. (*To himself.*) God, this is a mess.

(**FELIX** *enters again.*)

FELIX. Steamer's fine.

KELLY. Before we head back up, can I ask you something? Your sister...

FELIX. Excuse me?

KELLY. Nothin' like that. I was talking to her about her theory and –

FELIX. She bore you with that stuff?

KELLY. No. It's... It's pretty brilliant, actually.

FELIX. I'll be sure to tell her you think so.

KELLY. It's just... I'm surprised that it came from her. Not saying it shouldn't have it's just...with what happened earlier...

FELIX. It happens, ya know? It's been that way our whole lives. She was born that way. We uhhh... Ma didn't know there was two of us.

KELLY. How does that happen?

FELIX. I dunno, but it did. I was the expected one. But, we came early. Almost three months. I came out alright, my sister didn't.

KELLY. Jesus.

FELIX. She's fine now. Just... Sometimes she has problems.

KELLY. Just you and your mom to help?

FELIX. She has a therapist. But, us mostly, yeah.

KELLY. Where's your dad in all this?

FELIX. Riverside Cemetery in Cleveland.

KELLY. Oh.

(Pause.)

FELIX. You done askin' questions?

KELLY. I'm just tryin' to understand –

FELIX. Understand what? Why do you care?

KELLY. You want me to apologize? Fine. I'm sorry. I'm sorry I thought I was doing something good.

FELIX. What's good about stopping some random guy on the street?

KELLY. I didn't know you lived here. I thought you were breaking in.

FELIX. Your concern for the community is touching.

KELLY. I was doing my job.

FELIX. Thought you were off shift.

KELLY. Doesn't change what's right.

FELIX. So you assumed that I was breakin' into a random store... Why?

*(**KELLY** doesn't answer.)*

Say it. Put it in words. Why did you stop me?

KELLY. I know what you're trying to do. You're trying to bait me.

FELIX. Then bite. Why is it the right thing to do to stop me?

KELLY. I'm not playing into this, okay?

FELIX. It's a simple question.

KELLY. What's your deal, huh?

FELIX. Don't act like you don't know.

KELLY. I don't. Why don't you tell me, huh? Tell me what the hell my problem is, since you seem to know.

FELIX. You asked enough questions. I don't have to answer any. But, there is one thing I'm dyin' to know.

KELLY. Yeah?

FELIX. Yeah. What were you doing out there?

KELLY. That's a dumb question.

FELIX. Then answer it.

(Pause.)

KELLY. Getting drunk.

FELIX. Why? Ain't no bars open, so no need to be walkin' around wasted.

KELLY. I didn't go to a bar.

FELIX. Then where did you come from?

KELLY. Why does it matter?

FELIX. You tell me what you were doing out there, and I'll give you your gun back. You can leave and you can go do whatever the hell you wanna do. Go drink yourself to death for all I care. I don't care anymore.

*(**KELLY** doesn't answer. **FELIX** becomes irritated.)*

You're fine askin' questions about my sister and my dead dad / but the moment questions get rough for you, you shut up.

KELLY. I didn't know your dad was dead.

FELIX. Now you know. Okay? Twelve years ago, cleanin' up the streets like your boys in blue are suppose to, he gets shot by some folks who didn't like that. Broad daylight. Kids on the corner could describe the car, tell you the color of the piece of shit... And you know what we were told for years by the police department? There was nothing they could do for us. How the hell is there nothing you can do? We know who did it.

That asshole showed up at the funeral. But we say somethin', and we are told that there ain't a damn thing they can do. We have no proof. It was bullshit, still is. We had to move so we didn't have to see that bastard's face. So, you a cop? That's fine with me. But you want *my* help, then you gotta give me more than your word and select moments of silence.

KELLY. I'm not to blame for any of that. I'm sorry that they didn't help you, but they can't just go busting down someone's door without hard evidence.

FELIX. But you can shoot a guy for havin' too many parkin' tickets?

KELLY. There's more to it than that!

FELIX. I know that kid who got shot had warrants, but from what I heard, it's all for small stuff.

KELLY. It's not that simple.

FELIX. God, more bullshit! It is simple! They are shootin' the wrong people!

KELLY. You don't know what you're talking about, okay?

FELIX. And you do?

KELLY. Yes! I do!

(Silence falls between the two. **KELLY** *takes a deep breath, calming himself.)*

Look, when I get back on the job, I'll look into it for you, okay? I know some people in Cleveland, I might be able to get the case –

FELIX. I'm not askin' for your help.

KELLY. Goddamn it, kid! You complain we don't help but when I offer you won't take it.

FELIX. Why were you out there? Tell me why you were out there.

*(***FELICIA*** comes rushing down.)*

FELICIA. Twin? Felix, can I get some light?

(**FELIX** *shines the light on* **FELICIA**.)

FELIX. You shouldn't be down here. There's still folks not too far away from the shop.

FELICIA. What's takin' you so long?

KELLY. We were just finishing up.

FELICIA. Good. Hurry up. Radio says a big announcement is comin'.

FELIX. 'Bout what?

FELICIA. Mamma thinks they gonna release names.

KELLY. Shit. Go back up, Felicia.

FELIX. Don't tell her what to do.

KELLY. *(To* **FELICIA**.*)* We're almost done here, okay? We'll be up in a minute.

(**FELICIA** *looks to* **FELIX**. **FELIX** *gives a quick nod.*)

FELIX. We'll be up.

(**FELICIA** *turns and exits.*)

What the hell was that all about?

KELLY. Before we go back up there. We gotta talk.

(Lights down.)

Scene Five

(Lights up on the apartment. **ELLA** *sits at the table, smoking again. The TV is on, the voices of the* **REPORTERS** *mixing with the sound of the sirens outside.)*

REPORTER. *(Voice-over.)* Many wonder if the release of the names of the other officers involved has come too late. It is also unclear if any of them were present in the proceeding that lead to the failed indictment of Officer Roach.

> *(***FELIX*** bursts into the room. Before he can speak,* **ELLA** *raises her hand, keeping him silent.)*

Still, the chief hopes that this will lead to the mending of relations between the force and the citizens. We are getting word that the National Guard is on standby if the situation were to escalate.

ELLA. Turn that off, will ya?

> *(***KELLY*** enters the room slowly as* **FELIX** *flips off the TV.)*

Where's his gun?

> *(***FELIX*** goes to the chair, pulls the gun from underneath it.)*

You know he's a cop now. Give it to him.

FELIX. Ma.

ELLA. That's what you told him, right? You get proof, you give him his gun.

> *(***FELIX*** starts to unwrap the plastic from around the gun.)*

Don't worry 'bout all that. Consider it a kind of gift wrappin'.

> *(***FELIX*** takes the gun and hands it to* **KELLY**. **KELLY** *takes the gun and slips it into his*

waistband with a sort of comfortable motion that comes with practice.)

FELIX. Where is Felicia?

ELLA. In her room. Why don't you go check on her.

> *(ELLA gives FELIX a look, telling and heavy. FELIX moves closer to ELLA.)*

FELIX. What are you doin', Ma?

ELLA. I ain't doin' nothin'. I'm just gonna see Officer Holton out.

> *(FELIX looks back at KELLY, then exits toward the bedrooms.)*
>
> *(ELLA takes a long drag before putting her cigarette out.)*

KELLY. You mind if I use the phone before I go?

ELLA. I do mind, yes.

> *(ELLA stares at KELLY. KELLY sits on the couch.)*

You got what you needed. Your bag is right there. Nothin' stoppin' you from leavin' now.

KELLY. I need to make a call.

ELLA. Need to? Interestin'.

KELLY. I understand why you're upset.

ELLA. You do? Your empathy is deep, isn't it? Where was that same empathy a few weeks ago?

KELLY. I was doing my job.

ELLA. What scares you, Officer Holton?

KELLY. You don't have to call me that.

ELLA. I asked you a question, Officer. What scares you?

> *(KELLY doesn't answer. ELLA pulls out another cigarette.)*

When I first moved here, I figured it was far enough away to keep my son safe. Ya know, where we were there were folks who thought they ran the neighborhood. They lived a way I never understood, but it wasn't for me to get, ya know? I just knew what I had to protect, and that was my kids. That girl in there? She is stronger than any other person I ever met. Ever. First grade she uhh... She didn't have no friends. Her brother, a magnet for snot-nosed punks, but he had friends. And he would leave her in her room, barely talkin' most of the time, and he couldn't understand why she was the way she was. I saw a brilliant little girl who loved stories and songs, who would sing in moments when most people wouldn't dare. But, once she got out there? Silent. Almost held back because they thought she was mute. Then, Felix heard his friends makin' fun of her. You should have seen him. Protectin' her. It wasn't until then that he saw her for what she was. Misunderstood. Almost unrealized to other folks.

KELLY. What are you telling me –

ELLA. My biggest fear is that people will see my son the way everyone else sees my daughter. Unrealized. When your own kid grows up, you're gonna worry about him comin' home safe, but for different reasons.

KELLY. You weren't there, okay?

ELLA. But you were. You were there when that boy got shot.

KELLY. He was nineteen, not a boy.

ELLA. Every mother I know would argue you on that. Did you tell his ma that he isn't her boy? Did you tell them anything?

KELLY. I was told I couldn't.

ELLA. Did you want to? I'm guessin' that your captain's orders are the only thing that stopped you.

(**KELLY** *starts to unwrap the gun.*)

I'd rather you didn't.

KELLY. You want to know the truth?

ELLA. You willin' to tell it finally?

KELLY. We were just carrying out our warrants. He had outstanding tickets.

ELLA. Ten men for tickets?

KELLY. It was myself and one other at first. But, when we knocked on his door and he took off... It's protocol, okay? You run, we call it in. So we chased him and more and more men joined us. Most of 'em fall back but I stay on him and I call in where we are, askin' for someone to cut him off. They were just supposed to tackle him, take him down to the ground. I'm right behind him, he takes a right around a corner and...

(**KELLY** *stops, composing himself.*)

I've never had to fire my gun on duty. Neither had Officer Roach. But, he was scared, okay? He was scared and he freaked out and he shot him. That's the truth. He didn't mean to but he did it.

ELLA. And a boy is dead.

KELLY. Like I wanted that.

ELLA. Protect and serve, right?

KELLY. No one wanted it to happen. For you to think so is...

ELLA. You tellin' me what I think now?

KELLY. It's flawed, okay? Simple and basic and flawed.

ELLA. God, you have audacity, that's for sure.

KELLY. I didn't shoot the kid.

ELLA. You might as well have.

KELLY. No. Fuck that.

ELLA. Excuse me?

KELLY. You think that I enjoy serving warrants? That I had fun chasing down that kid? You're wrong if you think that. I didn't sign up for that.

ELLA. Why did you then?

KELLY. Because when my son was born I saw the world for what it really was. Shitty. You know, not a day goes by in this city without someone getting stabbed or left bleeding somewhere? I am doing my part to help this city. And yes, even people like you.

ELLA. Like me?

KELLY. I didn't mean it like that.

ELLA. Tell me, what did you mean?

KELLY. I don't know why you are mad at me. I didn't get your husband killed.

(**ELLA** *rushes to* **KELLY**, *anger boiling over.*)

ELLA. You loose-lipped bastard. You don't know a goddamn thing about my husband. You don't know a goddamn thing about me! One night with us and you understand us enough where you feel comfortable talking about my husband?

KELLY. I get it, okay?

ELLA. No. You don't. You don't understand what it's like to wonder if your son is gonna come home. Or what it's like to have to explain to your daughter that ain't nobody gonna be diggin' up her daddy's bones to hear his story.

KELLY. It was an accident, for Christ's sake!

ELLA. One that happens far too often!

KELLY. You ever think about how I might feel about this? How anyone else might feel about all of this? I saw the kid dying right in front of me. Officer Roach... your killer...shaking like a child. No, I didn't talk to the family, but I couldn't bring myself to do it even if I could. No one wants to look someone else in the face and say, "Yes, I'm part of the reason your son isn't gonna be at dinner tonight." You never stop to think that maybe I hate it just as much as you do. Maybe even more. You're right, I don't understand what it's like to wonder if my son is ever gonna come home. But what about my son wondering if I'm coming home? Where's the sympathy for him? You see me as this big bad wolf, but I can't stop seeing that kid's face. I called the ambulance, held his hand as they tried to stabilize him, and for all I know I'm the last face he ever saw. He was dying and I was only trying to do my job. Now, when I close my eyes I see him. Everywhere. So much that I can't even kiss my boy goodnight without seeing that kid's face. You all get to throw your rocks, break your windows, take the streets...but I don't get to scream? I don't get to hurt over any of this?

ELLA. We ain't breakin' windows 'cause we want to. We've done our screamin' and we ain't been heard yet. You gotta shake the walls sometimes if you wanna be heard so bad.

(**KELLY** *pulls back, stepping aside to himself.*)

This ain't the glorious revolution you seem to think it is. We ain't proud of this. Nobody should be. There are things that have been ignored for too long and, while you may not think so, when you scream people listen. Only thing is what you screamin' about ain't worth a damn.

KELLY. That's not fair.

ELLA. I'm not sayin' you ain't hurtin'. I'm sayin' you late to the party.

(Pause.)

KELLY. That isn't the way any of this was supposed to happen. I just wanted to go for a walk...clear my head.

ELLA. With a police-issued gun?

KELLY. It's not the department's. It's mine. You know, I went back to the place it happened and I... I tried to play it out again and again. I stood where Roach stood and I drew my gun. Over and over and I tried to get where he was, you know? He was scared of dying, but I'll admit I don't understand it myself. I mean, we got vests, ya know? Protection. This kid had baggy pants and a T-shirt. So I pull my gun and I think why he didn't shoot him in the leg, or shoulder or...anywhere else. But then I think, if I thought someone had a gun, I'd do whatever I thought would get me home to my kid. It's not until after it all that you start to wonder what it might be like to –

(Outside, loud chantings wells, louder than before, stopping **KELLY** *in the middle of his sentence. The sound of hundreds of people*

taking to the streets is muffled, but only slightly, by the closed window.)

*(**KELLY** crosses to the window, looking out of it.)*

KELLY. I wouldn't be surprised if they want my head right now. Posting my face all over the local news... You know, I'm not even supposed to be in this city.

ELLA. You ain't?

*(**KELLY** shakes his head.)*

KELLY. Was told to duck out until everything blows over.

ELLA. What didn't you?

KELLY. I don't know... Maybe I thought I could help in some way. I even started praying again. Haven't done that in years, but I thought it couldn't hurt. What do you think would happen if I went out there right now... just stood in front of the whole crowd.

ELLA. I don't even wanna think 'bout that. I think it's stupid and you'd be a fool to do it.

KELLY. I gotta do something.

*(**ELLA** finally lights her cigarette. She takes in a deep draw. She lets the smoke pour out of her mouth before lowering her head.)*

ELLA. When I first opened this place I figured I'd just fill a need, ya know? Used the insurance money for the down payment, figured I'd make somethin' out of my husband's death. But, I've turned away what seems like hundreds of thousands of dollars for one reason. I refuse to clean out blood. I ain't squeamish and I ain't scared of it. I just don't think it's right to wipe away proof of pain, ya know? Don't sit right with me that someone can be cut open and in one afternoon it can all be forgotten. Pain ain't supposed to work that way. It ain't supposed to be easily forgotten.

(A bullhorn is heard, countering the chants. Things like, "Return to your homes!" and

> *"The streets must be cleared, now!" can be heard.)*
>
> *(**ELLA** chuckles to herself, almost in disbelief.)*

I thought that National Guard stuff was just a bluff.

KELLY. Do you mind if I try to make a call again?

ELLA. Go ahead.

> *(**KELLY** takes the cell phone off the table, dials the number, and waits. This time, he connects.)*
>
> *(The chanting outside grows louder.)*

KELLY. Hey! No, Astrid, it's me. Yeah... No, I'm okay. How's my little... Can I talk to him? Yeah, I know it's late but I just... Yeah... Can you speak up? I can barely hear you...

> *(The bullhorn echoes back against the chants, more aggressive and more pointed. The chants don't back down, but seem to get closer.)*
>
> *(**ELLA** crosses to the window, peering out. Another billow of smoke leaves her lungs.)*

I know... I know it's late I just... I need to hear his voice okay? Why does it matter if I've been drinking? Let me talk to my goddamn son!

> *(Crash! A bright flash is seen and a loud pop is heard as tear gas canisters erupt in the street below. The chants turn to yells, people fleeing. Some rioters are clashing with the National Guard.)*
>
> *(Offstage, coming from the bedrooms, **FELICIA** screams. Her yells morph into crying. **ELLA** turns to go into the bedrooms.)*
>
> *(**FELIX** enters the room.)*

FELIX. Ma, I need –

ELLA. I'm comin' baby.

> *(**ELLA** exits.)*

(**FELIX** *stands, looking at* **KELLY**, *who is now yelling into the phone.*)

KELLY. Does it matter where I am right now?

(*Another loud bang from outside.* **FELIX** *crosses to the window.*)

FELIX. You got your gun, why don't you leave already?

KELLY. *(Ignoring* **FELIX**.*)* I want to talk to Eli, okay? Just... put him on the phone.

FELIX. Why aren't you out there with those guys in riot gear? Chasin' us down. Beatin' our heads in.

KELLY. Jesus, kid. Can't you see I'm on the phone?

(*Back into the phone.*)

Well, wake him up!

(*Gunfire is heard.* **FELICIA** *whimpers from offstage.*)

ELLA. *(Offstage.)* Come on, baby girl. It's gonna be okay.

FELIX. Leave! We don't want you here!

KELLY. I will, if you just give me a second, okay!

(*To the phone.*)

Hello? Hell... Fuck!

(**KELLY** *tosses the phone at the couch.*)

You couldn't wait five second for me to get off the fucking phone?!

FELIX. I don't want you here!

KELLY. I'm not going out there! Do you see what's happening?

ELLA. *(Offstage.)* Felix!

FELIX. It's all crashin' down, ain't it?

(*Sirens join the chaotic symphony of yells and screams outside. More loud bangs are heard.*)

KELLY. You should be with your sister.

FELIX. Are you leavin'?

FELICIA. *(Offstage.)* Twin! Felix, come here!

KELLY. I'll leave when everything calms down! Do you want me dead?

FELIX. I could ask you the same thing.

> *(Bang! A large explosion is heard, rising over the screams and the yells. The sky lights up for a moment, like meteors hitting the earth.)*
>
> *(**FELICIA** runs into the room, **ELLA** right on her heels.)*

ELLA. That felt close.

FELICIA. Why did you leave me?

> *(**FELICIA** runs to **FELIX**. **FELIX** embraces her. **ELLA** peers out of the window.)*

ELLA. Shit. Molotovs.

> *(**FELIX** breaks away from **FELICIA**, heading toward the front door.)*

KELLY. Where are you going?

FELIX. I'm gettin' them away from the store.

ELLA. To hell you are.

FELICIA. Stay here. Please. Stay with me.

KELLY. Listen to your sister.

> *(**FELIX** ignores him and makes for the door again. **KELLY** grabs him. They struggle. **FELICIA** watches on, clutching **ELLA**.)*

ELLA. Felix! Stop!

> *(**KELLY** grapples **FELIX** from behind before taking him down on the couch, face down.)*

FELIX. Get off of me! Get the fuck off of me!

KELLY. I can't let you go down there.

> *(**FELICIA** turns her head into **ELLA**'s chest. She starts to mumble dinosaur facts like before.)*

ELLA. Stop actin' like a goddamn fool, son! Don't you see what you're doin' to your sister?

FELIX. I ain't lettin' us die in this mess!

ELLA. That's not for you to decide!

>   (**FELIX** *struggles against* **KELLY** *before eventually giving up.*)

FELIX. Fine! Shit. Just get off me!

>   (**KELLY** *lets him go, cautiously.* **FELIX** *sits up slowly. Another loud bang.* **FELICIA** *reacts to it, clutching her mother tighter.*)
>
>   (**KELLY** *looks at* **FELICIA** *and* **ELLA**. **ELLA** *starts humming a small tune to her daughter, rocking back and forth in place.*)
>
>   (**KELLY** *grabs his gun, unwrapping it as he walks toward the door.*)

ELLA. You stay put too, damn it.

>   (**KELLY** *exits out the front door.* **ELLA** *looks at the door for a moment before continuing to hum and rock* **FELICIA**.*)
>
>   (*Three shots ring out from the other side of the door.*)
>
>   (*The humming stops, and* **FELICIA** *stops mumbling. For a moment, there is nothing but the sounds of the streets below.*)
>
>   (*The door opens,* **KELLY** *enters, closes the door, and stands with his back pressed against it.*)

KELLY. Warning shots.

>   (**FELICIA** *turns to* **KELLY**, *letting* **ELLA** *go for a moment.*)

FELICIA. No one hurt?

>   (**KELLY** *shakes his head.*)
>
>   (**FELICIA** *walks over to the couch and sits next to* **FELIX**, *leaning her head on his shoulder.*)

ELLA. Everyone done bein' idiots now?

> *(No one answers.)*

Everyone just…just sit.

> *(The cell phone rings next to **FELIX**. He picks it up.)*

FELIX. Hello?

> *(He listens for a moment before pulling it from his ear. He lifts it up, toward **KELLY**.)*

It's for you.

> *(**KELLY** stands, takes the phone, and wanders over to the dining room table.)*

KELLY. Hello? …Hey kiddo. How are ya?

> *(**KELLY** sits. He is quiet for a bit. He smiles.)*

No. I'm still here. I uhh…just wanted to hear you, buddy. How have you been?

> *(The sounds of the scuffle, while not as loud as before, still wage war in the background.)*

> *(The lights begin to fade on the house. The flames flicker outside the window, continuing to paint the room with yellows and oranges. Lights down, as the sound continues.)*

Scene Six

*(The sounds of the clash give way to the sounds of birds chirping outside. Morning light floods into the room through the window. Asleep on the couch is **FELICIA**, head where **FELIX**'s lap once was.)*

*(**KELLY** enters from the bedrooms, holding bags of clothes and heading out of the apartment toward the stairs. **FELIX** comes up from downstairs and almost runs into **KELLY**. They stare at each other a moment, until **KELLY** eventually steps aside, letting **FELIX** pass.)*

FELIX. Thanks.

*(**FELIX** walks inside. **KELLY** exits. **FELIX** crosses over to **FELICIA** on the couch. He taps her, softly rocking her to wake her up.)*

Felicia.

*(**FELICIA** swats his hand away. **FELIX** rocks her a bit harder. She groans and shifts.)*

FELICIA. *(Half-asleep.)* Noooo.

FELIX. The museum called.

*(**FELICIA** sits up.)*

FELICIA. What?

*(**FELIX** smiles.)*

FELIX. Time to get up. Got work to do.

*(**FELIX** walks back toward the bedrooms. **FELICIA** glares at him as he walks away. She starts to turn off the TV as **ELLA** pokes her head in from the kitchen.)*

ELLA. Baby girl, you up?

FELICIA. Barely.

ELLA. Come on in here and give me a hand.

(**KELLY** *enters again from downstairs.*)

KELLY. Morning.

> (**KELLY** *picks up some of the bags that are lying on the back of the chair and hanging around the space. He exits again, bags in hand.* **FELICIA** *watches him leave.*)

FELICIA. What's he doing?

ELLA. Helpin', like I asked you to come do.

FELICIA. We openin' today?

ELLA. Why wouldn't we?

FELICIA. Is it safe down there?

ELLA. People tend to be braver at night.

> (**FELIX** *enters from the bedrooms, wearing a button-up shirt and slacks.*)

FELIX. You awake now?

FELICIA. The museum didn't call, Felix.

FELIX. Naw.

FELICIA. Why would you say they called? That ain't funny.

FELIX. Calm down, okay?

FELICIA. What if something happened. Ma, do you know if something happened to the museum?

FELIX. Nothin' happened to the museum.

FELICIA. I wasn't askin' you. Ma!

ELLA. Everythin' is fine, baby girl.

FELICIA. Can I call 'em?

ELLA. After you eat.

FELIX. Ain't nothin' happened.

> (**FELICIA** *hits* **FELIX** *on the arm.*)

FELICIA. Punk.

ELLA. Breakfast is almost done. Felicia, at least clear your books off the table.

> (**FELICIA** *crosses to the table and grabs her books. She takes them and places them on the*

side of the couch. **FELIX** *goes to the window, looking out as he finishes dressing.)*

FELIX. You don't think it's too early to file a claim? What if tonight kicks everything back up?

ELLA. Even if it is, I want you to go talk to 'em. Find out what we gotta do to get all of this settled.

FELICIA. Why don't we close today. Everyone would understand.

ELLA. Still gotta bring in money, baby girl. Your college ain't gonna pay for itself.

FELICIA. I have to get in first.

ELLA. And you will. No worries.

*(**FELICIA** exits toward the kitchen. **FELIX** walks over to the TV and flips it on.)*

REPORTER. *(Voice-over.)* – Increased presence of police forces. The National Guard will help enforce the curfew already in place and the hope is that larger numbers of law enforcement will keep the damage to a minimum. After the break, we look at one school's effort to give back to those who have been victims of the riots. Stay tuned to your number one morning news crew.

*(**ELLA** walks into the room, holding a few plates of food.)*

FELIX. I ain't stayin' long enough to sit down. Wanna get down there before half the city is.

ELLA. Call ahead. Let 'em know you comin'.

*(**FELIX** looks on the table for his phone.)*

FELIX. You know where my phone is?

*(**ELLA** pulls her phone out.)*

ELLA. Call it. Lines have been clear all mornin'.

*(**ELLA** exits into the kitchen again. **FELIX** starts to dial the phone, walking away from the window. **KELLY** enters. The phone rings in his pocket. **KELLY** pulls the phone out and extends it to **FELIX**.)*

KELLY. Sorry about that. Must have forgotten.

> (**FELIX** *takes the phone from* **KELLY**. *He slides it in his pocket, grabbing a few bites of food off a plate, then heads for the door.*)

FELIX. *(Calling toward the kitchen.)* I'm gone, Ma! Tell Felicia I'll be back.

> (**FELIX** *exits through the front door.*)
>
> (**ELLA** *enters the room again, holding another plate of food.*)

ELLA. Breakfast, baby girl. Turn that TV off, will ya?

> (**FELICIA** *enters, sees* **KELLY**, *and stops for a moment. She crosses to the TV and turns it off.*)

FELICIA. Can I eat later? I'd like to get clean first.

ELLA. You can shower after you eat.

> (**FELICIA** *looks at* **KELLY**.)

FELICIA. I'd really rather shower first, Ma.

ELLA. Don't come complainin' to me when you eatin' cold food. You know eggs never reheat well.

FELICIA. I'll be fine.

> (**FELICIA** *exits toward the bedrooms.*)

KELLY. Tough kids in the morning.

ELLA. They can be stubborn.

KELLY. I thought they preferred steadfast.

> (**ELLA** *laughs to herself.*)

ELLA. You didn't have to help with things downstairs. We got everything under control.

KELLY. It's not a problem. I don't think you should open yet, though.

ELLA. I can't stay closed for too long.

KELLY. At least wait until you have glass on your doors. Make sure you can close them and actually lock them.

ELLA. I think the worst of it has passed.

KELLY. You never really know.

> *(A silence passes between them.* **ELLA** *reaches for her smokes but decides not to take one. She shuffles in her seat, leaning forward a bit.)*

ELLA. I'm so use to startin' over now I'm afraid I'll never finish anythin'. It took a while to get everything stable. Get Felicia comfortable. It feels like it's all about to change. She got into school late last week. That's when I got the letter anyway.

KELLY. Really? That's great.

ELLA. I haven't told her yet. Can't bring myself to. She thinks her brother is comin' with her. Haven't told her he ain't yet either.

KELLY. Why not?

ELLA. There is somethin' about us being together, ya know? Somethin' about me and my two kids runnin' this place that makes me really think that things are always… things are safer when we are together. This place, it ain't my dream. But dreams usually don't amount to nothin' nowadays. I look at her and I see how big her dreams are and I know that she ain't gonna reach 'em all. That she might have to come back here, havin' failed or fallen short. And I think maybe it's easier to just not let her go than to see her come back like that.

KELLY. Your daughter seems brilliant.

ELLA. She is. Smarter in ways I'll never be. But…in some ways she ain't. Neither is Felix. What's goin' on out there, it's destructive. It's downright ignorant, and I can see where the ignorance out-rules the intelligent. Together, those two kids make one hell of a team. But they won't be together forever. They know that, and I know that… I guess I worry is all.

> *(***FELICIA*** enters the room, still clothed as normal.)*

FELICIA. Hot water ain't workin' right now.

ELLA. You check the pilot light?

*(**FELICIA** shakes her head.)*

I'll be right back.

*(**ELLA** gets up and exits through the front door. **FELICIA** starts to exit, but **KELLY** stops her with his words.)*

KELLY. I've been thinkin' about your theory.

*(**FELICIA** doesn't turn to look at him.)*

You said that you thought it needed a bit more work. And, I don't know nearly as much about all of this as you do. But, I wanted to tell you what I thought might be missing.

*(**FELICIA** turns around, upset, about to speak.)*

Before you get all upset, just hear me out. I don't mean any disrespect by any of it. Just some ideas.

*(**FELICIA** pauses, then takes a seat where **ELLA** was.)*

We have the other five events, right? And, like you said, they all stem from this outside force. Something triggered the events. But, these events were, for the most part, unstoppable, right?

FELICIA. Right.

KELLY. But, this next event. Number six... It's reversible.

FELICIA. I don't think you understand how –

KELLY. Just...hear me out. You said that humans are going to cause the next great extinction event. That we are the next meteor or volcano to wipe everything out. What if we could change that? What if...by some amazing effort we could turn it around. We saved the panda right?

FELICIA. You are missing one important element. The desire to change.

KELLY. You don't think people want to change?

FELICIA. Why hasn't it happened yet if they do?

KELLY. They just have to be shown how to. I think that's the only thing I don't fully understand about your theory. There doesn't seem to be any –

FELICIA. Hope?

KELLY. Yeah.

FELICIA. I don't really see any space for it right now.

(**ELLA** *comes back into the room.*)

ELLA. Should be good now, baby girl. Just give it a few minutes.

FELICIA. Ma, do you think my theory is hopeless?

ELLA. I'm not sure I understand.

FELICIA. Kelly says that my theory don't have any hope.

ELLA. It does kinda paint a grim future, baby girl.

FELICIA. But, you don't think that's justified?

ELLA. I don't get where you comin' from today.

FELICIA. Why are you takin' his side?

ELLA. I'm not takin' anyone's side, baby girl. I'm just tryin' to understand.

(**FELICIA** *starts to get upset.*)

FELICIA. My theory is based on logic and facts. Logic and facts.

KELLY. Maybe there's more to it than those things.

FELICIA. Like what?

KELLY. I... I'm not really sure.

ELLA. Baby girl, you are gettin' yourself all worked up for nothin' okay? We discussed this, didn't we? How when you get into school people are gonna ask questions and how you should react, right?

(**FELICIA** *nods her head.*)

FELICIA. Yes, Ma. We did.

ELLA. This isn't how we respond, is it? Lashin' out like that?

FELICIA. No, Ma.

ELLA. Well now. Go take your shower, okay? Try to calm yourself a bit. We'll talk more about it later.

(**FELICIA** *nods her head.*)

FELICIA. Sorry, Kelly.

KELLY. No need to apologize. It was my fault.

ELLA. Go on, now.

>   (**FELICIA** *exits toward the bathroom again.*)

You see what I mean? It's gonna be different for her out there.

KELLY. That's not a bad thing. Not always.

ELLA. You get deep in the mornin', don't you?

>   (*They both chuckle.*)

You know what thought is kinda frightnin'? That this is all that I have. When I'm gone, this is all I'm leavin' behind. And Felix already knows that this is what my legacy is gonna be. This cleaners on this corner in this neighborhood. But that might not even amount to nothin'. Not with everything burnin' down around us.

KELLY. I told Felix I would help find who killed your husband.

ELLA. Ain't nothin' to find. I could point the fool out as he walked out of a 7-Eleven. I ain't worried about findin' him no more.

KELLY. Why not?

ELLA. I'm still livin' ain't I? They both still breathin'. Yeah, they angry about it. But, I kinda like that in 'em. Both of 'em. Keeps 'em sharp. Lets them know this world don't owe them nothin', and it ain't about to hand nothin' over either. Not for free.

KELLY. I honestly don't understand.

ELLA. Wouldn't expect you to. Can I tell you somethin' I ain't never told Felicia? I think you're right about her theory.

KELLY. How it's hopeless?

ELLA. Yeah. All doom and gloom and boom with no light at the end of any tunnel. No way out. And it's flawed because of that. But, I think she is pointin' her ideas in the wrong direction. What is happenin', out there? Ain't the first time it has. I sure as hell hope it's the last, but I ain't stupid enough to think long enough on that idea. You know what's being wiped out, faster than anything else in this place? Doin' what's right. People who seem to give half a damn enough to even stand up for somethin'.

KELLY. What about all those people out there last night?

ELLA. They are standin' up for somethin', but I'm not sure they even know fully what they are pullin' for. What changed last night? Seems like next to nothin'.

KELLY. There are good people out there. You, me.

ELLA. Two of us.

KELLY. Your husband…

ELLA. They vanishin' day by day. My husband, he was a good man. He was doin' what's right. Believed in it until the day he died. My son wants nothin' more than to do what's right, like his daddy. But, what does the world show him? That "right" gets you nowhere. I'm not tryin' to blame you. If anything, from what I've seen you are one of those being wiped out too.

KELLY. That still sounds hopeless to me.

ELLA. It ain't though. You and your son… I heard the softness in your voice. The way you talk to my daughter like she means somethin' to you. Not everyone has that. I'm leavin' behind this store, seein' as I don't have nothin' else but this. I've prayed over my kids, I've taught them what I can and I feel at some point the world has gone and taken so much goodness away from them. Felix don't see it like his sister does. He can't see the sun on days like today. He sees the burnin' cars and the smashed windows. I can't give him anything but smashed windows now.

KELLY. But that isn't your fault. I see nothing but smashed windows too.

ELLA. Ain't you supposed to see more than that? What about why they broken?

KELLY. I don't see that. Not anymore. My son… Hopefully my son will see it like you do. Like Felicia does. But, I don't think I can. I used to look at a broken window and see how it let in more light. But, I don't anymore.

ELLA. I think you might have just proved her theory after all.

(**FELIX** *comes through the front door.*)

FELIX. Got ahold of the insurance company. They ain't open today. I don't think we should be either.

ELLA. Can't afford to stay closed, you know that.

FELIX. There's somethin' we gotta take care of.

KELLY. Ella, I don't... How did I prove her theory?

ELLA. You are bankin' on time that not all of us have, alright?

KELLY. Time? What time?

FELIX. What are you two talkin' about?

ELLA. Officer –

KELLY. I don't see what you see in your son. Believe it or not, I see a young man who has the level of pride in his father that I hope my son has for me. Just because he sees the window as smashed doesn't mean he's broken. Never did. You have lost things I can never understand, and there are things that cannot be replaced. There is anger here. And, I get it.

ELLA. You won't ever really get it.

FELIX. Ma. Can I talk to you?

KELLY. You're right. Maybe I won't. But does that mean I should stop trying?

FELIX. Why are you still here?

ELLA. Don't be rude, Felix.

FELIX. And you ignoring me is, what?

KELLY. Because I'm trying to do some good.

FELIX. Both of you, shut up.

(*Both* **ELLA** *and* **KELLY** *fall silent.*)

It's bad out there, okay? Not sure how much work we gonna be able to get done today. But we gotta get him out of here.

KELLY. What?

ELLA. He's right. You can't stay.

KELLY. I understand you're putting yourself at risk with me being here, so I'll leave. I promise. But I have to know...

(*To* **ELLA.**)

What would you have me do? I can't change all of this. I can't fix everything. I'm stuck in the middle like you are, only I feel like I don't have a way out.

ELLA. But you do. You can stop being a cop. You can stop being seen as those guys with bullhorns and tear gas. We can't stop being black. Trust, many have tried. But it don't change the fact that your idea of us is different. I'll admit, it ain't always bad...but it's different. You know the difference between last night and 1992? The backdrop. I've seen this before. And now I've lived through it. My kids have lived through it. You know what that's like? No. You don't. You still have the option to fade into the background while we have to live with the reality. For the first time, you can't be unknown.

Your face is everywhere. For a second... I had some pity for ya. Some deep and stirring pity. But, now you get to live like we do. You don't get to hide. Not no more.

FELIX. Ma, we can't keep him here.

ELLA. I know, son. But the officer asked me a question.

KELLY. You insist on calling me that. Why?

ELLA. You want to make a difference? Do somethin' with the title. Don't hide from it or run from it. Do somethin' with it.

KELLY. Like what?

ELLA. Do they know that you sat in the ambulance with that boy?

KELLY. No.

ELLA. Why not?

KELLY. I don't know...

ELLA. Then seems like you know where to start.

(**ELLA** *reaches for his bag on the side of the couch.*)

You got your gun?

(**FELICIA** *comes bursting into the room, clothed but wet.*)

FELICIA. There isn't any hope in my theory because that's not what it needs. It needs change.

ELLA. What?

FELICIA. We have the ability to see patterns, order from chaos, signs of what's gonna come, right? Within that ability is the chance to break things down and see the cause of those patterns, the chaos. That allows us to find the inciting event and avoid it. So, my theory doesn't need hope with the understanding that application of the theory is set to the current model.

FELIX. What the hell are you talking about?

FELICIA. Doom comes when we don't change. My theory works in its current state because there are no signs of widespread change. The factor, hope, isn't hope at all. It's humanity. But, humanity hasn't changed enough to upset the current predicted outcome.

(**FELICIA** *is excited and huffing.*)

I need to call the museum. Tell them what I've found. Do you think that I can resubmit an updated version of my theory? I'll have a better chance of getting into school if I do.

ELLA. Baby girl, you don't have to worry about it.

FELICIA. I do. If Kelly saw the hole in my theory, then I'm sure they will.

ELLA. Go into my room.

FELICIA. You aren't listening.

ELLA. Top drawer of my dresser. Pull out the letter right on top, okay? Felix, go with her.

(**FELIX** *knowingly smiles. He crosses to* **FELICIA**, *grabbing her by the arm and taking her back toward the bedrooms.*)

KELLY. What happened to not telling her yet?

ELLA. That girl's gonna change things. I can't let her keep thinkin' this might be all she has.

KELLY. It wouldn't be so bad if it was. It's more than I've got.

ELLA. Nothin' wrong with what you got. Not when you know how to fix it.

KELLY. I don't.

ELLA. Ain't you heard a word that girl said?

> *(A high-pitched squeal comes from offstage.* **FELICIA** *comes running in, holding her acceptance letter in hand.* **ELLA** *throws her arms open and they embrace, spinning around.)*

I'm so proud of you, baby girl!

FELICIA. Can Felix come with me to orientation?

FELIX. I'll be there, twin.

> *(***FELICIA*** hugs ***FELIX*** tightly. ***KELLY*** stands, watching. He smiles a bit, grabbing his bag. ***FELICIA*** looks at him.)*

FELICIA. Where are you going? You... You can't leave now.

ELLA. Baby girl, he can't stay here.

FELICIA. But...he hasn't finished his breakfast.

FELIX. He can't stay.

> *(***FELICIA*** crosses over to ***KELLY***. She gives him a hug. ***KELLY*** hesitates for a moment, then hugs her back. ***FELICIA*** pulls back, struck by an idea.)*

FELICIA. Does your boy like dinosaurs?

> *(Before ***KELLY*** can answer, ***FELICIA*** takes off to the bedrooms.)*

ELLA. I guess she's right. Stay for breakfast, at least.

KELLY. I'd like to stay long enough to help clean up downstairs, if that's okay. I want to help.

ELLA. We'll talk about it, okay? Felix, call Flora and tell her not to come in today. We ain't ready to open back up yet.

FELIX. I thought we decided that he has to leave.

KELLY. I'll be gone before the end of the day. Might be easier to get me out at night anyway.

> (**FELICIA** *runs back in, dinosaur toys in hand.*)

FELICIA. These aren't actually all that correct. We've learned a lot more about their physical makeup since these were made and –

ELLA. Baby girl, don't bother him right now. After he eats.

KELLY. No. It's fine. I don't mind. Let's not do it at the table, okay? Let your brother and mother eat.

> (**KELLY** *takes some of the toys and walks over to the couch.* **FELICIA** *follows him, happily.* **FELICIA** *begins to point out certain things on the toys that are now incorrect, and* **KELLY** *nods in confirmation that he understands.* **FELIX** *sits down where* **KELLY** *was.* **ELLA** *switches the plates of food, giving him a fresh plate.*)

ELLA. It's okay, Felix. He ain't doin' nothin'.

FELIX. What are you doin', though?

ELLA. What your father would've. Switch on the radio, will ya?

> (**FELIX** *looks at* **ELLA**. *She gives him a stern "now" look. He sighs, flipping on the radio. Soft sounds of jazz fill the space.* **KELLY** *walks to the table, grabs the plate he was eating off of, and takes it to the couch where* **FELICIA** *is sitting. He nibbles a bit as she continues to explain things about each toy.* **FELIX** *begins to eat, but then pulls out his phone. He dials.*)

FELIX. Hey, Flora. Yeah, don't come in today. Store won't be open. Gotta fix a few things. Might take a while. Come by on Monday. Things should be better by then.

*(**FELIX** hangs up the phone, starting in on his food again. The sound of the birds and the city beginning to start again mingle with the jazz music in the space. Lights begin to fade.)*

(Blackout.)

End of Play

www.ingramcontent.com/pod-product-compliance
Lightning Source LLC
Chambersburg PA
CBHW051410290426
44108CB00015B/2231